Table of Contents

Getting Started .2
Inside a Museum 4
Kinds of Museums 8
Museums to Visit 12
Index 16

by Carol K. Lindeen

Getting Started

Have you ever seen a real dinosaur? Of course not, because dinosaurs are **extinct**! But maybe you have seen a dinosaur's bones in a **museum**. A museum is a place where you can see all kinds of interesting things that teach us about our world.

Museums come in all sizes, and they can show us many different kinds of things. A museum can show us how people lived and worked long ago. A museum can even show us models of what life might be like in the future!

Many museums have **displays** that you can touch and play with. Some displays are made just for kids. In fact, some museums are built just for kids! Museums can be a lot of fun to visit. Let's learn more.

Inside a Museum

When you go into a museum, it might have free **admission**, or you might need to buy a ticket. You might want to get a map of the museum's **floor plan**, so you don't get lost. A floor plan shows where to go to learn about things like dinosaurs, mummies, or prehistoric tools.

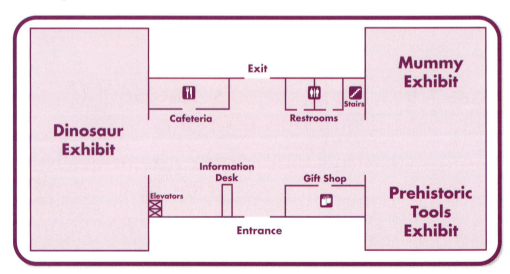

A floor plan of a museum

Some museum displays are kept behind ropes or bars. The ropes are there to help protect the display from being broken. They are also there to help protect visitors like you. The museum caretakers don't want visitors to be unsafe in the museum.

Some objects in museums are kept in glass cases. Very old objects, like this ancient pottery, are **fragile**. That means they can break easily. A glass case helps keep objects safe so that everyone can enjoy them.

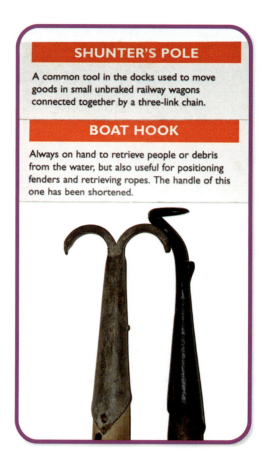

Many museum displays have signs that tell you about the **artifacts**. The signs might say where or when the artifact was found. You might also learn what the artifact is made of or how it was used.

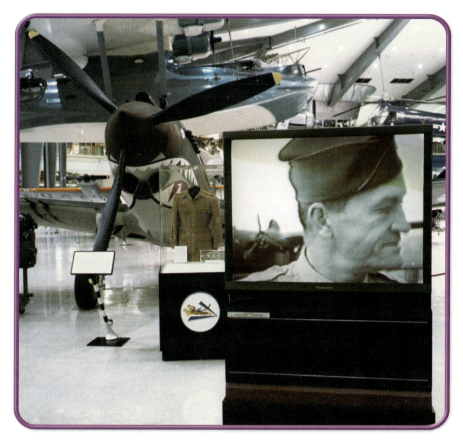

Sometimes museums have audio recordings to listen to. You can put on headphones, press a button, and hear about a special display. In some museums, visitors can watch movies or videos.

Kinds of Museums

An art museum is full of paintings, sculptures, and many other kinds of artwork, often from all over the world. Some of the art may be very old, and some of it may be brand new. You might see things like jewelry, dishes, furniture, and clothing from faraway places or from places close to home.

Some of the things in an art museum are the works of very famous artists. But in the very same museum, you might find art made by people with unfamiliar names. Some things on display may even be the work of unknown artists who lived long ago.

An art museum might have just one kind of artwork, such as art from Asia. Some art museums are filled with artwork by just one artist. And sometimes the museum building itself is a work of art!

Science museums teach us about how things work. You might learn about how sound travels or how electricity works. You might get to look through a microscope. You might walk through a model of your heart, or see a film about Mars.

At a natural history museum, you can see things like fossils, bones, and life-size models of animals. You can learn about people from cultures that predate our time. You can uncover all kinds of facts about life in the past.

Museums to Visit

If you want to visit a museum, you will find many different kinds in many different places. You might find museums that feature sports and games or toys and dolls. You might find a train museum, a car museum, or an airplane museum. You can find museums in big cities and in small towns.

Visiting a museum is a fun thing to do with your family. It's a great way to learn new things about new places. Many museums have Web sites. You can explore the Web site ahead of time to print out a floor plan and preplan your visit.

The Smithsonian Institution is made up of many different museums. Most of them are in Washington, D.C. One of these museums, the National Museum of Natural History, has a big African elephant inside.

The Metropolitan Museum of Art

Many cities have famous museums. The Metropolitan Museum of Art is in New York City. It has three huge floors of art from all over the world. Some U.S. cities that have exciting science museums are Atlanta, Boston, Chicago, and San Francisco.

    A visit to a large museum in a big city can take up a whole day! But smaller museums can be just as much fun to see. Maybe you can visit a museum close to where you live.

Index

art, 8, 9, 14

artifact(s), 6

bones, 2, 11

dinosaur(s), 2, 4,

display(s), 3, 5–8

floor plan, 4, 12

fossils, 11

Metropolitan Museum of Art, 14

natural history, 11, 13

paintings, 8

pottery, 5

science, 10, 14

sculptures, 8

Smithsonian Institution, 13